PARACLETE PRESS

PO Box 1568

Orleans, MA 02653

We hope you will enjoy this book and find it useful in enriching your life.

Book title: _____

Your comments: _____

How you learned about this book: _____

Reasons why you bought this book: *(check all that apply)*
❑ Subject   ❑ Author   ❑ Attractive Cover   ❑ Attractive Inside
❑ Recommendation of Friend   ❑ Recommendation of Reviewer   ❑ Gift

If purchased: Bookseller _____ City _____ State _____

Please send me a Paraclete Press catalog. I am particularly interested in: *(check all that apply)*

1. ❑ Spirituality
2. ❑ Spiritual Practices (Which ones?) _____
3. ❑ Theology
4. ❑ Prayer/Worship
5. ❑ Catholic Inspiration
6. ❑ Orthodoxy
7. ❑ Fiction
8. ❑ Religious Traditions (Which ones?) _____
9. ❑ Other _____

Name (PRINT) _____
Street _____ City _____ Phone _____ State _____ Zip _____
E-mail _____

Please send a Paraclete Press catalog to my friend:

Name (PRINT) _____
Street _____ City _____ Phone _____ State _____ Zip _____

PARACLETE PRESS
PO Box 1568 • Orleans, MA 02653 • Tel: 1-800-451-5006 • Fax: 508-255-5705
Available at better booksellers. Visit us online at www.paracletepress.com.

God
under my
ROOF

God under my Roof

Celtic Songs & Blessings

ESTHER DE WAAL

PARACLETE PRESS
BREWSTER, MASSACHUSETTS

2006   First Printing This Edition

Copyright © 1984, 2006 by The Sisters of the Love of God
ISBN 1-55725-516-4

First published in 1984 by SLG Press, Oxford, England
First Paraclete Press edition published in 1985; this edition
published 2006.

Library of Congress Cataloging-in-Publication Data

De Waal, Esther.
  God under my roof : Celtic songs and blessings / Esther de
Waal.
      p. cm.
  Originally published: Orleans, Mass. : Paraclete Press,
1985, c1984.
  ISBN 1-55725-516-4
  1. Prayers. 2. Christian poetry, English. I. Title.
  BV245.D45 2006
  242'.80089916--dc22

                                            2006014007

10 9 8 7 6 5 4 3   2 1

Published by Paraclete Press
Brewster, Massachusetts
www.paracletepress.com
Printed in the United States of America.

TABLE OF CONTENTS

THE GREAT
GOD OF LIFE

THOMAS MERTON tells the story of the Zen master who asked a postulant presenting himself at the monastery gate, "Why do you seek such a thing [i.e. the truth about Zen Buddhism] here? Why do you wander about neglecting your own precious treasure at home?" (*Thomas Merton on Zen,* Introduction by Irmgard Schloegl, 1976, p. 54). It is a parable that we would do well to take to heart, for it suggests the relevance of our interest in these treasures of the Celtic tradition. Why do we wander about neglecting our own precious treasure at home [in the United Kingdom]? Recent years have seen the enormous growth in exploration of other religious traditions, particularly those of the East; yet have we not failed to recognize

3

the wealth of a tradition much nearer to us, a tradition "at home" in our own native islands? Why do we not seek our "precious treasure" very literally "at home"? Every form of spiritual exercise or new therapy derived from the East, or even from the West, is seized on with excitement, but the possibility of finding God in our everyday lives, in the prosaic and the mundane, has not caught the popular imagination with any excitement.

These Celtic prayers and poems (the two are inseparable since to ask God for his blessing is already to have acknowledged his gift), the legacy of the simple farming and fishing people in the Hebrides, are shot through with an awareness of God's presence that can speak to men and women of today. Their sense of God's immediacy in daily living is precisely what so many people are urgently searching for today, as they struggle to acquire techniques of "mindfulness" or to practice the contemplative approach in daily living. The self-conscious approach of our contemporaries would, of course, have been totally alien to a people who found it entirely natural to see God in every moment and at every level of their ordinary life. They walked with God, with Mary and the saints, addressing them tenderly and familiarly, and involving them in whatever they were doing. The material things of daily life almost inevitably became a way to God for a people who always speak of soul and body with equal respect and for whom the borderline of secular and sacred seems irrelevant. Their prayers were songs, and as they crooned or intoned them, they seem close to the continuous prayer the Orthodox describe as a murmur in the heart.

It is always easy to pursue parallels between religious traditions, and it would not be difficult to find much in common not only with Orthodoxy but also with the Hebrew attitude to man or with Eastern teaching on "awareness." But it is a more creative exercise to let these poems speak for themselves. They come from a people with their own particular genius, and it will be sufficient if they explain themselves to us as a gift of grace, if they can touch our hearts and enrich our vision. It is not my intention here to enter into any academic, historical or theological discussion of the Celtic tradition which these poems reflect. Anyone who wishes to pursue the subject further may enjoy the anthology which I published with A.M. Allchin, *Daily Readings for Prayers & Praises in the Celtic Tradition*, Templegate Publishers, Springfield, Illinois, and also selections from the Carmina Gadelica which I edited in *Celtic Vision*, St. Bede's Publications, Petersham, Mass. For an overall discussion of Celtic Christianity see *Every Earthly Blessing*, *Rediscovering the Celtic Tradition*, Servant Publications, Ann Arbor, Michigan and *The Celtic Way of Prayer, the Recovery of the Religious Imagination*, Doubleday, New York, 1997.

The poems we will be considering, the *Carmina Gadelica*,[1] come from the outer Hebrides, the rocky, remote and far-flung islands off the northwest coast of Scotland which were the home of a hardy pastoral and sea-going people.

They were collected by an amazing scholar, Alexander Carmichael, who for the last forty years of the nineteenth century lived amongst these people, collecting and transcribing what had belonged hitherto to an entirely oral tradition. Like many of the greatest translators, Carmichael himself was a poet. His English renderings from the Gaelic are not only faithful, but "their grandeur and power show him as one of the translators through whom a masterpiece can be reborn in a new language" (Adam Bittleston, *The Sun Dances, Prayers and Blessings from the Gaelic,* 1960, xi). Since many of those to whom he listened were already well-advanced in years, much of the material in the *Carmina Gadelica* would now be almost certainly two hundred years old, though Carmichael would claim that much went back to the seventeenth century, and also contained even older elements.

The pattern of life in the outer Hebrides up to the present century when evictions, emigration and education changed everything drastically, was simple. Here were crofting and fishing communities in which men and women worked hard by day and in the evenings gathered together to talk and to sing. Poetry was central to their life, poetry carried on from generation to generation by word of mouth. Carmichael said of these people: "Mirth and music, song and dance, tale and poem pervaded their lives as electricity pervades the air." *(Carmina Gadelica,* I, xxxiii.) He found simple old men and women in lowly homes addressing "the great God of life, the Father of all living" in words which were at once homely and eloquent, presenting to him their needs and desires, fully and familiarly, and yet also with awe and deference.

There was little in their poetry of what is popularly assumed to characterize something Celtic, something typically misty or mystical, or vaguely pantheistic. Rather these Gaelic people found it quite natural to bring into their prayers and poems the vigour, honesty and incisive humour of their daily lives. What also in particular makes these poems unique is that, unlike the much better known bardic poetry, "these poems are private; they reveal what is not usually revealed to strangers and outsiders." (G.R.D. McLean, *Poems of the Western Highlanders,* SPCK 1961, xxvii.) Carmichael tells of an episode in which one old man, having allowed him to take down a "going to sleep" rune, traveled twenty-six miles the following morning to see him again and to exact a pledge that his "little prayer" should never be allowed to appear in print. "I should not like cold eyes to read it in a book." (*Op. cit.,* IV, xxxi.) Carmichael therefore destroyed it (and it is lost to us, as is so much of this rich treasury—stamped out, destroyed, dispersed).

Although certain of these songs or prayers—and it is significant that it is impossible to draw any distinction between the two—were designed for communal gatherings and rituals, most were meant to be sung privately, intoned softly or crooned secretly. Catherine Macphee, a cottar, after giving Carmichael a night-shielding poem, described how the women sang these verses at the time of going to sleep; then she added: "the people of that day were full of hymns and prayers, full of music and songs, full of joy and innocent merriment. By the Book itself, you would not ask but to be hearing them, however long the night, however wild the weather, however miry the road, however dark the night going homeward." (*Op. cit.*, III, 350-1.)

Perceiving a world in which the divisions of sacred and secular seemed irrelevant, these Gaelic people found God lovingly concerned with all aspects of their lives and felt themselves walking not only in his presence but close to the saints and angels too. Almost as a matter of course they assumed that they were surrounded by a multitude of spiritual beings, near throughout the day and nearer still in the hours of sleep. The involvement of the saints, and above all, the involvement of Mary and Michael, Columba and Brigit, was taken for granted and forms a constant subject of great numbers of poems.

The holy apostles' guarding,
The gentle martyrs' guarding,
The nine angels' guarding,
    Be cherishing, be aiding me.

The quiet Brigit's guarding,
The gentle Mary's guarding,
The warrior Michael's guarding,
    Be shielding, be aiding me.

The God of the elements guarding,
The loving Christ's guarding,
The Holy Spirit's guarding,
    Be cherishing, be aiding me.
        (III, 106-7)

1. *Carmina Gadelica, Hymns and Incantations with Illustrative Notes of Words, Rites and Customs Dying and Obsolete:* Orally collected in the Highlands and Islands of Scotland by Alexander Carmichael, see acknowledgment. References given in this study are to volume and page number.

COMMON
CREATION

AN AMAZINGLY POWERFUL VISION of the
universe is expressed in these poems. The sense
of a common creation is experienced so strongly
that sun and moon, animals and crops are also
felt to have the need to receive a blessing. The
encompassing of the Trinity and the saints is not
confined to man alone. The unity of God and his
saints, the whole created order, man, beasts and
growing things is continually assumed. An old
man in Arasaig would take off his head covering
and bow when he saw the sun each day, thanking
the great God of life for the glory of the sun and
for the goodness of its light to the children of
man and to the animals of the world. When the
sun set in the western ocean the old man would

again take off his head covering and would bow
his head and say:

> I am in hope, in its proper time
> That the great and gracious God
> Will not put out for me the light of grace
> Even as thou dost leave me this night.
> (III, 308-9)

At the sight of the new moon another old man
told Carmichael, "A person ought to make rever-
ence to it and make the cross of Christ over the
tablet of his heart, and to say the rune in the eye of
the God of glory who sees all."

> He who created thee
> Created me likewise;
> He who gave thee weight and light
> Gave to me life and death.
> (III, 304-5)

It is interesting to see expressed the feeling of *common* creation. However this is very far removed from any sort of easy-going, romantic pantheism. At the heart of this sense of unity lies the recognition that everything good comes from God and is to be given freedom to be itself, to enjoy and be enjoyed, and that we are enslaved if we care for anything in ways that exclude the Giver (A. Bittleston, *op. cit.*, p. xv). The song of a woman on Harris who cured herself of leprosy by using aright the healing plants and fish demonstrates this frame of mind:

> It were as easy for Jesu
> To renew the withered tree
> As to wither the new
> Were it His will to do so.
> > Jesu! Jesu! Jesu!
> > Jesu! meet it were to praise Him.

There is no plant in the ground,
But it is full of His virtue,
There is no form in the strand
But it is full of His blessing.
    Jesu! Jesu! Jesu!
    Jesu! meet it were to praise Him.

There is no life in the sea,
There is no creature in the river,
There is naught in the firmament
But proclaims His goodness.
    Jesu! Jesu! Jesu!
    Jesu! meet it were to praise Him.

There is no bird on the wing,
There is no star in the sky,
There is nothing beneath the sun
But proclaims His goodness.
    Jesu! Jesu! Jesu!
    Jesu! meet it were to praise Him.
                (I, 38-41)

Children learning the first prayer of the day from their mothers were unconsciously made to feel their worship of God took place in the midst of the whole worship of the natural world. "My mother would be asking us to sing our morning song to God down in the back-house, as Mary's lark was singing it up in the clouds, and as Christ's mavis was singing it yonder in the tree, giving glory to God of the creatures for the repose of the night, for the light of the day, and for the joy of life" (III, 25). The dressing prayer she was taught as a child set the keynote for the rest of the day, which is seen as a total act of worship both in activity and in word:

I am giving Thee worship with my whole life,
I am giving Thee assent with my whole power,
I am giving Thee praise with my whole tongue,
I am giving Thee honour with my whole
utterance.

(III, 44-5)

19

Amongst the many morning prayers comes this one, typical in its lifting up all things to God at the start of the day, an act of affirmation since they have come to man through the love and bounty of God:

Each thing I have received, from Thee it came,
Each thing for which I hope, from Thy love it will
    come,
Each thing I enjoy, it is of Thy bounty,
Each thing I ask comes of Thy disposing.

                           (III, 58-9)

This is nowhere better expressed than in the long morning prayer from an old woman, Mary Gillies, which starts with a great credo:

I believe, O God of all gods,
    That Thou art the eternal Father of life,

and goes on to list his attributes: Father of love, of the saints, of each one, of mankind, of the world, of the high heavens and the skies and the oceans. Then this great credal affirmation turns into an act of worship, wherein the totality of the individual person responds to this vision of God the creator:

I am giving Thee worship with my whole life,
I am giving Thee assent with my whole power,
I am giving Thee praise with my whole tongue,
I am giving Thee honour with my whole utterance.

I am giving Thee love with my whole devotion,
I am giving Thee kneeling with my whole desire,
I am giving Thee love with my whole heart,

I am giving Thee affection with my whole sense,
I am giving Thee my existence with my whole
   mind,
I am giving Thee my soul, O God of all gods.

(III, 44-5)

The wholeness of each human being is utterly central to their thought. A man prays, "O bless myself entire" (III, 38), since to ask for a blessing on the soul without it also being a blessing for the body would never occur to him:

Make Thou my prayer availing
   To my soul and to my body.
         (III, 78-9)

Body and soul are juxtaposed throughout:

Give us, O God, the needs of the body,
   Give us, O God, the needs of the soul;
Give us, O God, the healing balsam of the body,
   Give us, O God, the healing balsam of the soul.
         (III, 386-7)

A morning prayer might take the form of a consecration:

> Consecrate us
> Heart and body
> Thou King of Kings, Thou God of all.
>   Amen.
>
> Each heart and body
> Each day to Thyself,
> Each night accordingly,
> Thou King of Kings, Thou God of all.
>   Amen.
>
> (I, 18-21)

Accepting the unity of body and soul together naturally leads to an acceptance of the work of the hands, and this morning prayer includes the phrase "the handling of my hand," an attitude at the start of each day which is basic to the work that follows:

Bless to me, O God,
> My soul and my body;
Bless to me, O God,
> My belief and my condition;

Bless to me, O God,
> My heart and my speech;
And bless to me, O God,
> The handling of my hand.

Strength and busyness of morning,
Habit and temper of modesty,
> Force and wisdom of thought,
And Thine own path, O God of virtues,
> Till I go to sleep this night;
Thine own path, O God of virtues,
> Till I go to sleep this night.

(III, 26-7)

The day ends similarly with this night prayer:

> Father, bless me in my body,
>> Father, bless me in my soul.
> Father, bless me this night,
>> In my body and my soul.
>>>> (III, 348-9)

A prayer for peace carries this thought a stage further, for it asks that peace may be:

> Upon each thing my eye takes in,
> Upon each thing my mouth takes in,
> Upon my body that is of earth
> And upon my soul that comes from
>> on high.
>>>> (III, 264-5)

From this wholeness within the self comes a readiness to be open towards the whole universe, and to be receptive to the people and the things of that universe, with all the five senses:

Bless to me, O God,
  Each thing mine eye sees;
Bless to me, O God,
  Each sound mine ear hears;
Bless to me, O God,
  Each odour that goes to my nostrils;
Bless to me, O God,
  Each taste that goes to my lips,
  Each note that goes to my song,
  Each ray that guides my way,
  Each thing that I pursue,
  Each lure that tempts my will,
  The zeal that seeks my living soul,
The Three that seek my heart,
  The zeal that seeks my living soul,
The Three that seek my heart.

(III, 32-3)

THE PROTECTING
PRESENCE

A SENSE OF AWE does not exclude a sense of the familiar, so that in their prayer men and women approach God in their own terms: He is helmsman at sea and herdsman on land, as well as being their chief.

> Be Thou with us, O chief of chiefs,
> Be Thou Thyself to us a compass-chart,
> Be Thine hand on the helm of our rudder,
> Thine own hand, Thou God of the
>   elements,
> Early and late as is becoming,
>   Early and late as is becoming.
>   (I, 326-7)

"And as country people knowing much of the medicinal property of plants and with many charms and incantations for healing, they find it quite natural to assume that he is as skilled and familiar in these arts as they are themselves." So amongst the prayers for protection comes this:

> Put Thy salve to my sight,
> Put Thy balm to my wounds,
> Put Thy linen robe to my skin,
>> O Healing Hand, O Son of the God
>> of Salvation.

(III, 82-83)

Thus the sense of God's actual presence is immediate and when a blessing asks, "Be Thy right hand of God under my head" (I, 88-9) it is no abstract expression. The day ends with a night-blessing:

I lie in my bed
As I would lie in the grave,
Thine arm beneath my neck
 Thou Son of Mary victorious.
     (I, 94-5)

And if by chance that night's sleep should turn into
the death-sleep, then God's arm will still be there:

Be it that on Thine own arm,
O God of Grace, that I in peace shall
 waken.
     (I, 84-5)

This constant sense of the close presence of God
at every point both on life's journey and on the
day's journey is the theme of poem after poem:

God before me, God behind me,
God above me, God below me,
I on the path of God,
God upon my track.

Who is there on wave?
Who is there on billow?
Who is there by door-post?
Who is along with us?
   God and Lord.

I am here aboard,
I am here in need,
I am here in pain,
I am here in straits,
I am here alone,
   O God, aid me.

                              (III, 318-9)

Often each person of the Trinity will be asked to play a specific role in protecting:

Be the eye of God dwelling with you,
The foot of Christ in guidance with you,
The shower of the Spirit pouring on you,
   Richly and generously.

                              (III, 204-5)

A son or daughter leaving home would receive the mother's blessing at the outset of a journey for which the urgent need of God's protection and of the continuing presence of the Trinity were felt more keenly than ever.

The keeping of God upon thee in every pass,
The shielding of Christ upon thee in every path,
The bathing of Spirit upon thee in every stream,
In every land and sea thou goest.

(III, 246-7)

THE HANDLING
OF MY HANDS

THE DEDICATION OF TIME, of night and day, of the day's journey, is part of the great affirmative under-standing of God and man, and of the created world, within which it is inevitable that the material of everyday life should be seen as a way to God. Getting up and dressing, kindling the fire and milking the cow, driving the herds or grinding the corn, all become occasions for prayer and for finding the presence of God. "Bless the handling of my hands" is the summation of prayers by which from dawn to dusk, from rising to sleeping, men offer themselves and their work to God who will consecrate them, body and soul, and all their labours. As water cupped in the hand is splashed over the face at the start of the day, this prayer is made to the Trinity:

The three palmfuls
Of the secret Three
To preserve thee
From every envy
Evil eye and death;
The palmful of the God of Life,
The palmful of the Christ of Love,
The palmful of the Spirit of Peace,
    Triune,
    Of grace.

                        (I, 62-3)

The prayer at dressing assumes body and soul together seek blessing:

O great God, aid Thou my soul,
    With the aiding of Thine own mercy;
Even as I clothe my body with wool,
    Cover Thou my soul with the shadow of Thy
        wing.

                      (III, 30-1)

For the woman, "lifting" the peats is the first duty of the day, and as she kindles the fire, the saints and Mary and Christ himself are all involved most immediately in what she is doing:

> I will build the hearth
> As Mary would build it.
> The encompassment of Bride and of Mary,
> Guarding the hearth, guarding the floor,
> Guarding the household all.
>
> Who are they on the lawn without?
> Michael the sun-radiant of my trust.
> Who are they on the middle of the floor?
> John and Peter and Paul.
> Who are they by the front of my bed?
> Sun-bright Mary and her Son.
>
> The mouth of God ordained,
> The angel of God proclaimed,
> An angel white in charge of the hearth
> Till white day shall come to the embers.

An angel white in charge of the hearth
Till white day shall come to the embers.

(I, 236-7)

In another poem the action takes on a wider significance, for the fire becomes symbolic of the flame of love which we should keep burning for the whole family of mankind.

I will kindle my fire this morning
In the presence of the holy angels of heaven,
In the presence of Ariel of the loveliest form,
In the presence of Uriel of the myriad charms,
Without malice, without jealousy, without envy,
Without fear, without terror of any one under
the sun, But the Holy Son of God to shield me.
Without malice, without jealousy, without
envy,
Without fear, without terror of any one
under the sun,
But the Holy Son of God to shield me.

God, kindle Thou in my heart within
A flame of love to my neighbor,
To my foe, to my friend, to my kindred all,
To the brave, to the knave, to the thrall,
O Son of the loveliest Mary,
From the lowliest thing that liveth,
To the Name that is highest of all.

(I, 230-1)

Of all the labor-songs that mark each successive task, it is in those for milking that we see most vividly how completely at home the woman feels with Christ, with Mary and the saints:

> Come, Mary, and milk my cow,
> Come, Bride, and encompass her,
> Come, Columba, the benign,
> > And twine thine arms around my cow.

> Come, Mary Virgin, to my cow,
> Come, great Bride, the beauteous,

> Come, thou milkmaid of Jesus Christ
>> And place thine arms beneath my cow.
>>> (I, 270-1)

As she sits and croons lilts and lullabies, poems and prayers, with cow after cow until all are milked, she asks for a blessing not simply upon her hands but upon the teats that she is handling:

> Bless, O God, my little cow
>> Bless, O God, my desire;
> Bless Thou my partnership
>> And the milking of my hands, O God.

> Bless, O God, each teat
>> Bless, O God, each finger;
> Bless Thou each drop
>> That goes into my pitcher, O God.
>>> (IV, 64-5)

Sometimes the four teats themselves will be addressed by name:

The teat of Mary, the teat of Bride,
The teat of Michael, the teat of God
    divine.

(IV, 62-3)

As she churns the milk for butter, she finds it natural to turn to the saints who are standing nearby for their practical aid:

Come thou Brigit, handmaid calm,
    Hasten the butter on the cream;
See thou impatient Peter yonder,
    Waiting the buttered bannock white and yellow.

Come thou Mary, Mother mild,
    Hasten the butter on the cream;
See thou Paul and John and Jesus
    Waiting the gracious butter yonder.

(IV, 86-7)

Loom blessings were important in a world in which the woman would spend much of her time weaving cloth for her household:

My warp shall be very even,
Give to me Thy blessing, O God,
And to all who are beneath my roof
In the dwelling.

(I, 296-7)

These daily chants became much more elaborate when, on Saturday night, she would stop weaving and carefully tie up the loom and suspend a cross or crucifix above the sleay:

Bless, O Chief of generous chiefs,
My loom and everything a-near me,
Bless me in my action,
Make Thou me safe while I live.

In the name of Mary, mild of deeds,
In the name of Columba, just and potent,
Consecrate the four posts of my loom
Till I begin on Monday.

Every web, black, white and fair,
Roan, dun, checked and red,
Give Thy blessing everywhere,
On every shuttle passing under the thread.

Thus will my loom be unharmed
Till I shall arise on Monday:
Beauteous Mary will give me of her love,
And there shall be no obstruction I shall not
   overcome.

(I, 304-5)

"Waulking" the cloth, that is stretching it on a frame to strengthen and thicken it, was a communal activity which gave rise to waulking songs sung by a group of women who joined together for this purpose. One of them, the consecrator or celebrant, would lead a ceremony at sunrise, placing the roll of cloth in the centre of the frame, turning it slowly and naming each member of the household for whom it was intended, then reversing it in the name of Father, Son and Spirit.

Not only is the woof and warp and every thread thus consecrated to God, but also the final process takes place in his presence, and he is even assumed to be participant in the action, placing his arm around each woman as she waulks (I, 296-7).

Quern songs, like all the labor-songs, were composed in a measure which reflected the work itself, a measure which changed to suit the rhythmic motion of the body at work. The woman would sit on the floor to grind, filling and relieving the quern with one hand and turning it with the other, while singing to the sound of the revolving stone (I, 252-3). This song, made up of very short lines, looks forward to the good times ahead:

> We shall have mead,
> We shall have spruce,
> We shall have wine,
> We shall have feast.

> (I, 256-7)

THE PATH
OF GOD

As the men set out for their day's work, leaving home to fish or farm, they would say a short prayer, singing or intoning it sometimes in an almost inaudible undertone. They could assume the companionship of God with such confidence that they were actually laughing as they went:

> My walk this day with Christ
> My walk this day with Spirit
> The Threefold all-kindly
> Ho! ho! ho! the Threefold all-kindly.

> My shielding this day from ill,
> My shielding this night from harm,
> Ho! ho! both my soul and my body,

Be by Father, by Son, by Holy Spirit,
By Father, by Son, by Holy Spirit.

Be the Father shielding me,
Be the Son shielding me,
Be the Spirit shielding me,
    As Three and as One:
    Ho! ho! ho! as Three and as One.
                    (III, 48-9)

So much time, particularly for men, was spent in journeying, in driving the animals, in walking to the fields, that journey prayers are common. Journeys always become a time for them to walk with God and for God to walk with them. The presence of God, always keenly felt, is here seen in a most practical, immediate sense.

I on Thy path, O God
Thou, O God, in my steps.
                    (II, 158-9)

> God, bless the pathway on which I go,
> God, bless the earth that is beneath
>   my sole.
>
>   (III, 178-9)

Those lines from a journey prayer were used however short the distance or small the errand. Time and again the songs follow a similar form:

> Bless to me, O God
>   The earth beneath my foot,
> Bless to me, O God,
>   The path whereon I go.
>
>   (III, 180-1)

There are many herding songs which the men sang as they drove their cows and sheep to pasture. Everyone knew that the King of Shepherds would watch over both men and flocks as he had always done, to protect them from the many dangers of the hills and bring them safely home. So this was a common refrain when talking to the animals:

Be the herding of God the Son about your
    feet,
Safe and whole may ye home return.

(I, 276-7)

Sometimes God is not simply herdsman, but also
friend: "the friendship of God the Son" to bring
them home, with "lovely Mary keeping them"
and Christ himself at the end of their way. When
a man had brought his flock to the pasture in the
morning, he would take leave of them tenderly,
waving his hands towards them in patriarchal
blessing and commending them to the keeping of
Christ and the saints:

The herding of Bride to the kine,
Whole and well may you return.

The prosperity of Mary Mother be yours,
Active and full may you return.

The safeguard of Columba round your feet,
Whole be your return home.

Be the bright Michael King of the angels
Protecting, and keeping, and saving you.

The guarding of God and the Lord be yours
Till I or mine shall see you again.

The herding of the fair Mary
Be about your head, your body, and aiding you.

(I, 272-3)

In the yearly cycle of work the preparation of seedcorn was important and certain rituals were always observed. Three days before the actual sowing, the seed would be sprinkled with clear, cold water in the name of Father, Son and Spirit, the moistening of the seed hastening its growth. This would generally be done on a Friday, which was held to be an auspicious day for all operations except those involving the use of iron (the connection being made here, of course, with the nails of the Cross). The farmer begins thus:

> I will go out to sow the seed,
> In the name of Him who gave it growth;

He continues,

> Every seed will take root in the earth,
> As the King of the elements desired.

But, as always, he is aware of the saints standing alongside to help him in his work:

> I will come round with my step,
> I will go rightways with the sun,
> In the name of Ariel and the angels nine,
> In the name of Gabriel and the Apostles
>   kind.
> Father, Son and Spirit Holy,
> Be giving growth and kindly substance,
> To everything that is in my ground,
> Till the day of gladness shall come.
>
> (I, 244-5)

On the day when they were to begin the reaping, the whole family dressed in their best and went out to the fields to hail the God of the harvest. The father cut the first handful of corn, laid his bonnet on the ground and, facing the sun, waved the handful of corn three times, sun-wise, round his head as he sang the reaping salutation, which the family would then take up, praising the God of the harvest who gave them food and flocks, corn and clothing, health and strength, peace and plenty (I, 240-7).

> God, bless Thou Thyself my reaping,
> Each ridge, and plain, and field,
> Each sickle curved, shapely, hard,
> Each ear and handful on the sheaf.
> Each ear and handful on the sheaf.

Bless each maiden and youth,
Each woman and tender youngling,
Safeguard them beneath Thy shield of
    strength,
And guard them in the house of saints,
Guard them in the house of saints.

(I, 246-7)

But while the seasonal changes play their part, ultimately it is the individual response to the pattern of daily living, expressed in ritual response to morning and evening, which comes across most forcefully in the poems. As "lifting" the peats had been the first duty of the day, so smothering or "smooring" is the last. It is an action which is made symbolic and is performed with loving care, the peats being divided into three sections, one for each Person of the Trinity. The first peat is laid down in the name of the God of Life, the second the God of Peace, the third the God of Grace. The circle is then covered with ashes, enough to subdue but not to extinguish the fire, in the name of the Three of Light. When this has been done, the woman closes her eyes, stretches her hand and softly intones one of the many smooring prayers:

> The Sacred Three
> To save
> To shield
> To surround
> The hearth
> The house
> The household
> This eve
> This night
> O! this eve
> This night
> And every night
> Each single night.
> Amen.

(I, 234-5)

The bed-blessings which bring the day to its close
are amongst the most powerful, and also the most
characteristic, of these poems. It was difficult to
think of sleep without death, and impossible to
think of either except in terms of the continuing
presence of God and the saints. These poems
speak vividly, tenderly and securely of what that
presence means:

I am lying down to-night as beseems
In the fellowship of Christ, Son of the Virgin of
    ringlets,
In the fellowship of the gracious Father of glory,
In the fellowship of the Spirit of powerful aid.

I am lying down to-night with God,
And God to-night will lie down with me,
I will not lie down to-night with sin, nor shall
Sin nor sin's shadow lie down with me.

I am lying down to-night with the Holy Spirit
And the Holy Spirit this night will lie down with
   me,
I will lie down this night with the three of my love,
And the three of my love will lie down with me.

(I, 82-3)

     I lie in my bed
     As I would lie in the grave,
     Thine arm beneath my neck,
     Thou Son of Mary victorious.

     Angels shall watch me
     And I lying in slumber,
     And angels shall guard me
        In the sleep of the grave.

     Uriel shall be at my feet,
     Ariel shall be at my back,
     Gabriel shall be at my head,
        And Raphael shall be at my side.

Michael shall be with my soul,
The strong shield of my love!
And the Physician Son of Mary
Shall put the salve to mine eye,
 The Physician Son of Mary
 Shall put the salve to mine eye!
    (I, 94-5)

GOD IN
OUR MIDST

THESE CELTIC PEOPLE lived quite naturally and quite unselfconsciously in a state of prayer, a state of prayer whose daily and yearly rhythm was dictated not by daily office or yearly lectionary, as in the monastic tradition, but by the demands of a hard-working existence. Thus their prayer responded to, and grew out of, life itself with all its relentless demands. They had found that the pattern of daily living could become the most natural way to God. Here we come face to face with a profound truth, a truth which though so often enunciated yet needs to be repeated time and time again: God uses the common material things of life to reveal himself—bread and wine and water. In the wilderness it was manna fallen from heaven and water struck from the rock which reminded the Hebrews of God's present reality. In the New Testament frequently it was at a meal of some sort that people met Jesus. So, not only are material things good in themselves, they are also signs of the present activity of God, and they can, if we will let them, open up a relationship to him. So God in fact comes to us where we are, at home.

For thirty years Jesus lived a hidden life at Nazareth with Mary and Joseph, working as a carpenter, taking his part in home and community. Jean Vanier has reminded us that before we begin to talk about any idealized "good life," or impose upon ourselves demanding (and probably guilt-inducing) spiritual challenges, we should try to live out our own lives as Jesus lived out that hidden life, "living all that makes up daily life tenderly and competently" (Jean Vanier, *Community and Growth*, 1979, p. 220). A life of prayer which grows directly out of activity and is not an escape from it, is a form of contemplative prayer which more and more people are seeking urgently. We need help in order to unearth God in our midst so that the awareness of his constant presence (together with the saints) is mediated through daily work and not destroyed by it.

What the poems and blessings of the Celtic people can renew in us is a vision which in our time has become narrowed, impaired, even lost entirely. Much in their lives that was humdrum, back-breaking, unrewarding may seem to us romantic, colored by our nostalgia for their simpler and less complex world. Much of what they were doing does not begin to be applicable to our style of life today or to its pressures and demands. Of course this is so, and it would be foolish to deny it. Yet that should not be allowed to blind us to the truth that it was their *attitude* of accepting, enjoying, rejoicing over, transforming whatever lay to hand that was at the heart of their religious experience. The mundane was the edge of glory. Loving God does not demand the heroic and the unusual. "Work is love made visible" says Kahlil

Gibran, and love is not doing the extraordinary but knowing how to do the ordinary things in our life. So work and love and praying and life are inseparable, just as the prayer and poetry are inseparable—a truth so simple and so profound that we should carry it with us, as these poems do, from morning to evening, from year's beginning to year's end, from birth to death.

God's Aid

God to enfold me,
    God to surround me,
God in my speaking,
    God in my thinking.

God in my sleeping,
    God in my waking,
God in my watching,
    God in my hoping.

God in my life,
    God in my lips,
God in my soul,
    God in my heart.

God in my sufficing,
    God in my slumber,
God in mine ever-living soul,
    God in mine eternity.

(III, 52-3)

Encompassing

The compassing of God and His right hand
Be upon my form and upon my frame;
The compassing of the High King
    and the grace of the Trinity
Be upon me abiding ever eternally,
    Be upon me abiding ever eternally.

May the compassing of the Three shield me in my
    means,
The compassing of the Three shield me this day,
The compassing of the Three shield me this night
    From hate, from harm, from act, from ill,
    From hate, from harm, from act, from ill.
               (III, 102-3)

Peace

    Peace between neighbors,
    Peace between kindred,
    Peace between lovers,
        In the love of the King of life.

    Peace between person and person,
    Peace between wife and husband,
    Peace between women and children,
        The peace of Christ above all peace.

Bless, O Christ, my face,
 Let my face bless everything;
Bless, O Christ, mine eye,
 Let mine eye bless all it sees.

(III, 266-7)

A Mother's Blessing

Be the great God between thy two shoulders
To protect thee in thy going and in thy coming.
Be the Son of Mary Virgin near thy heart,
And be the perfect Spirit upon thee pouring—
Oh, the perfect Spirit upon thee pouring!

(II, 170-1)

Augury

I am going without
To the doorship of my house
    In the holy name of God
Stronger of sight than all.

I go out in the name of God,
    I come in in the name of the Son
I walking in Thy path, O God,
    Thou, O God, upon my doorstep.

God before me, God behind me,
God over me, God beneath me,
God within me, God without me,
    The God of marvels leading me.
                   (V, 296-7)

Bed Blessing

I am lying down tonight
With Mary mild and with her Son,
With the Mother of my King,
Who is shielding me from harm.

I will not lie down with evil,
Nor shall evil lie down with me,
But I will lie down with God,
And God will lie down with me.

(I, 88-9)

ESTHER DE WAAL is an Anglican laywoman, writer, mother of four sons. Her special interests lie in the fields of Benedictine and Celtic spirituality. Her *Seeking God, the Way of St. Benedict* (Liturgical Press, Collegeville, Minnesota), written while she was living in Canterbury, has become a worldwide bestseller. In 1988 she edited a selection from the *Carmina Gadelica, Celtic Vision* (St. Bede's Publications, Petersham, Mass.). Her most recent book is *The Celtic way of Prayer, the Recovery of the Religious Imagination* (Doubleday, New York, 1997). She has now returned to the Welsh Border country where she grew up as a child, though she also travels widely, lecturing and giving retreats.

ACKNOWLEDGMENT

Thanks are due to the Scottish Academic Press, Edinburgh, for kind permission to quote extensively from *Carmina Gadelica, Hymns and Incantations, with Illustrative Notes of Words, Rites and Customs Dying and Obsolete:* Orally collected in the Highlands and Islands of Scotland by Alexander Carmichael; Vols. I and II by Professor James Carmichael Watson and Vols. V and VI edited by Professor Angus Matheson.

About Paraclete Press
Who We Are

Paraclete Press is an ecumenical publisher of books and recordings on Christian spirituality. Our publishing represents a full expression of Christian belief and practice—from Catholic to Evangelical, from Protestant to Orthodox.

Paraclete Press is the publishing arm of the Community of Jesus, an ecumenical monastic community in the Benedictine tradition. As such, we are uniquely positioned in the marketplace without connection to a large corporation and with informal relationships to many branches and denominations of faith.

We like it best when people buy our books from booksellers, our partners in successfully reaching as wide an audience as possible.

What We Are Doing
Books

Paraclete Press publishes books that show the richness and depth of what it means to be Christian. Although Benedictine spirituality is at the heart of all that we do, we publish books that reflect the Christian experience across many cultures, time periods, and houses of worship.

We publish books that nourish the vibrant life of the church and its people—books about spiritual practice, formation, history, ideas, and customs.

We have several different series of books within Paraclete Press, including the best-selling *Living Library* series of modernized classic texts; *A Voice from the Monastery*—giving voice to men and women monastics about what it means to live a spiritual life today; award-winning literary faith fiction; and books that explore Judaism and Islam and discover how these faiths inform Christian thought and practice.

Recordings

From Gregorian chant to contemporary American choral works, our music recordings celebrate the richness of sacred choral music through the centuries. Paraclete is proud to distribute the recordings of the internationally acclaimed choir Gloriæ Dei Cantores, who have been praised for their "rapt and fathomless spiritual intensity" by *American Record Guide*, and the Gloriæ Dei Cantores Schola, which specializes in the study and performance of Gregorian chant. Paraclete is also the exclusive North American distributor of the Monastic Choir of St. Peter's Abbey in Solesmes, France, long considered to be a leading authority on Gregorian chant performance.

Learn more about us at our website:
www.paracletepress.com, or call us toll-free at
1-800-451-5006.

Sacred Spaces
Stations on a Celtic Way
Margaret Silf
192 pages, ISBN: 1-55725-278-5
$23.00, Hardcover, illustrated

"For all of us, the only beliefs to which our deepest heart and soul can consent are those which our personal experience endorses. Sacred spaces are opportunities to meet that experience and allow it to take us beyond itself. And then to discover for ourselves what the mystery we call life means for us and where it is drawing us." —Margaret Silf

The Celts believed that the visible and invisible worlds, the material and the spiritual, were one. Certain places, such as hilltops, groves, and springs, were sacred, and in those places the presence of the spiritual was almost palpable. In this book, Margaret Silf introduces seven traditional sacred spaces, and invites us to reflect on their meaning in our own lives.

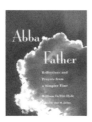

Abba Father
Reflections and Prayers from a Simpler Time
William Dewitt Hyde
Edited by Hal M. Helms
73 pages, ISBN: 1-55725-200-9
$6.95, Trade Paper

Written while the author hiked the Swiss Alps, the twenty-two prayers and meditations in this volume encourage us to seek God in the ordinary events of life and in the beauty of the natural world. They touch on many facets of life including love, bereavement, work, responsibility, courage, humility, and hope. Combining beautiful imagery with spiritual revelation, *Abba Father* will be cherished by those who want to begin to pray and by those who want to refresh their prayer life.